ISBN 978-1-0980-7129-5 (paperback)
ISBN 978-1-0980-6664-2 (hardcover)
ISBN 978-1-0980-6665-9 (digital)

Christian Faith Publishing, Inc.
832 Park Avenue
Meadville, PA 16335
www.christianfaithpublishing.com

Instagram
Jimmy Pallavicini
rocket_juice

Printed in the United States of America

Wine
and
Love

JIMMY J. PALLAVICINI

Her Taste

A glass filled with words.
There's much in her eyes.
The wine brings out magic.
Syrah and Merlot,
a blend that's so heavy.
In color, it shows.
She's smooth and fruit forward,
her eyes, feel like home.
She bites on my lips,
and that's how I know.
A wine that's so true,
Syrah and Merlot.
The energy's something,
something I know.
I hold her hand,
a kiss on the go.

Your Eyes, Darling

I taste the beauty of the heavens here on Earth.
It's not the wine, but a feeling in the soul,
when you look into my eyes and I look into yours.

Love of Mine

I heard some whispers in a dream.
She said, your eyes are meant for me.
It's something in the heart and soul.
She said, you're what I'm looking for.
I love you, mama, on and on.
Today, tomorrow,
moon and sun.

Words for Two

I spoke some words of wisdom.
May the light come shine on through.
May we always be protected,
our air, our sun, our moon.
May the waters keep on moving.
May the soul feel like it's new.
Protection is protection,
always from me to you.

One Flower

A flower in my dream.
When I wake, I can see clearly.
There's kisses to my soul,
her eyes give me much more.
I'm a man, and I am king.
She's energy of day,
a beauty of the sun.
So many lovely flowers,
but the truth, I just see one.
She has something about her.
I'm something of the wise.
I take a drink of Mezcal,
and I'm going with the flow.
Today and my tomorrow,
my love is always yours.

Colored Blue

The beauty of my words
are written just for you.
I'm poet of a dream,
a man,
I'm my own king.
I can pick a thousand flowers,
but none compare to you.
Your eyes, they have a birthmark.
Your soul is colored blue.
Your voice is my desire.
I hear you in a dream.
You whisper words of love,
like you're my everything.
Your heart, your mind, your soul.
I'm here for you, my darling.
My queen, you are today.
I love you, *mi amor*.

A Sip of You

An eagle and a pen,
a flower and a crown.
Two hearts are full of passion.
Your voice, a lovely sound.
There's nothing in the cold,
so have some Chardonnay.
The flowers, they all love me.
Your eyes, they have me stay.
There's moonlight in the rain,
a kiss of Chardonnay.
I walk into the forest,
with a uniform of gray.
I tell you, love of mine,
a magnet to the soul.
Today and my tomorrow,
a kiss, our lips, our all.

Blue Skies

I speak about the beauty
of the sky and of your eyes.
I can see they both have blue.
I looked up and thought of you.
In your eyes, the sky has magic,
like a kiss onto the soul.
It's your heart that calls my name,
it's a kiss that sparked the flame.
It's everything about you,
like a magnet to the soul.
I love you, pretty mama.
Your eyes, your lips, your all.

The Eagle

An eagle picks a flower,
and brings it to his queen.
The keys to every kingdom are his,
but she's his dream.
The grapes out in the vineyard
are always part of him.
La Rioja's in his blood.
The wine of every king.
The beauty of a moment.
Be wise and live a dream.
It's God that gives him strength,
and love that brings him in.

12

Beauty of the Soul

My thirst is heavy
when I look into her eyes.
The kiss she gives me,
is beauty of a kind.
Like fine Merlot,
it gets into the soul.
The stars are shining.
The Moon, it has a glow.
The taste is smooth,
like kisses to the soul.
I like this lady,
Merlot, Merlot, Merlot.

Your Kisses

I can kiss you, darling.
Beautiful you are.
I can hold you tight,
a flower to the heart.
Moonlight always wishes,
protects, and guides the soul.
Your kisses are Merlot,
and Merlot is what I know.

Blended Soul

She's got eyes that were made by lightning in the sky.
Eyes of beauty, an energy so bright.
Tell me, mama, do you hear the song?
Sunshine flowers, kisses on and on.
You're the beauty that makes the glass so full.
I'm the wine blended with the soul.
Kisses, darling, always so you know.

To My God

I've spoken to my God,
he saved me once or twice.
By that I mean, a couple hundred times.
I know from wrong and right, and the balance to it all.
Be strong, and I'll be stronger.
Her heart, her smile, her soul.
Forever and forever protection, so you know.

She's More

All around, the sunshine kissed her soul.
There's beauty in the magic.
I'm sun, I'm air, I'm all.
She's more than just a rose.
Her eyes are of the sky.
Her heart is full of light.
Her kiss is of fine wine,
wine that's of my kind.
My lovely señorita,
I'm with you for all time.

Meadow

There's flowers in the meadow,
and then some old oak trees.
The grapevines keep on budding.
The sun brings out more leaves.
I feel it in the soul,
her eyes I've known before.
She tells me with her smile,
that she's the one for me.
It's something in her eyes,
the beauty that I see.
Her lips, her heart, her voice.
Darling, you and me.

1452

I appreciate the beauty of the moonlight in the sky.
When I have a glass of wine,
it's her kisses every time.
Her eyes, I've known before,
like a magnet to the soul.
We must have met each other back in 1944.
Or maybe much, much longer, like in 1452.
Whatever time it was,
her eyes are always blue.
And I always know it's her,
through her kiss, her voice, her smile.
And we always share a wine,
it's our thing for all of time.
Sweet Virginia blue,
a wine for me and you.

Full Moon

The moonlight I see clearly,
a recharge to the soul.
She gives me light and passion.
The moonlight knows it all.
There's stars and different colors,
like a birthmark in the sky.
Refreshing is the air,
today and till all time.

Rosé

Your color is beauty,
a light cherry red.
You taste like the heavens,
I'm laying in bed.
I drink you and notice,
that you make me smile.
There's no one like you for miles and miles.
Here in the valley they grow my Syrah.
They made you a rosé,
I like you a lot.
You're smooth with bright flavors,
you land on my lips.
Your taste is so smooth,
a velvety kiss.

My Wine

I respect her in her nature,
a vine of Chardonnay.
She has the eyes of beauty
that grab a hold of me.
I can see into the future,
a bottle that's so true.
It's winter, and I have a thought for me and you.
The flowers bloom in spring,
the sunshine tells a story.
When I look into her eyes,
she gives me strength and glory.
I can see into her roots,
like I knew her long ago.
A vine that has the fruit,
a wine that tastes like home.
It starts off in the spring.
The process of great wine,
the energy comes natural.
A kiss, our lips, our time.

24

Within the Soul

The shadow of the wine is dark,
the color's burgundy.
An angel dances,
giving warmth and light to me.
Radiating beauty,
a very lovely wine.
Brilliant in color,
her taste is more than fine.
The kisses that she gives me
are a light within the soul.
The Moon is getting brighter,
and there's beauty with it all.
I have to say I love her.
She's my darling, *mi amor*.

One Love

Her eyes are made of beauty,
like the sky and pink Merlot.
They have a lovely birthmark,
the gate into her soul.
Her voice gives out a tune,
and I want her more and more.
I'm poet of a dream,
and I've lived just like a king.
I've also seen the hardships of one too many things.
I've lived a thousand lives and won so many wars.
I've loved you all my life.
You're everything, *amor.*

The Seasons

There's a feeling that I'm after,
like a pocket full of words.
I know all of her beauty.
I'd change nothing of hers.
Like the sun onto a flower.
Like wine in every dream.
There's nothing more enchanting.
Her eyes are what I mean.
She's winter and she's summer.
She's autumn and she's spring.
Her voice, her smile, her kisses,
I know she's everything.

Hearts Fire

I'll have tequila on the rocks.
With lime and mineral water.
I like my Cabernet with hints of plum.
It's just my style.
I like my calamari with tentacles, my friend.
I'm thinking of the sand, the beach,
and her sweet smile.
I like my queen with eyes
that do something to my soul.
I like her voice to be everything I'm looking for.
I like to see the owls flying late at night.
I like a balance in my world to feel perfectly right.
I like to go to places
with a lovely Spanish sound.
I like to write about my darling,
her eyes, her heart, her kiss, and smile.

Flower Blue

The vines, the flowers,
and always the sun.
The moon I desire,
my love, only one.
To find you is natural,
a smile on your face.
Your eyes are of beauty,
and your lips know my taste.
I love you so much.
There's magic in us.
It comes and it comes,
this love within us.

All Day

Wine, good food, and music.
Friends that chat away.
Looking out the window,
sunny sky today.
Thinking of a challenge,
stronger day and day.
Reaching for the next step.
Words that find a way.
Magic in the heavens,
dreams of you at night.
Talking to the future,
knowing time is right.
Gold coins in my pocket,
spirit of a king.
Looking out the window,
back into a dream.

Rain

The rain brings new beginnings,
and freshens with its touch.
The flowers keep on blooming,
yellow mustard lush.
The grass does seem much greener,
and the trees have no more thirst.
The earth has settled down,
and created puddle clones.
I walk around and feel refreshed,
and have a deeper thought.
Of beauty in this nature,
the raindrops make a splash.
My instincts of a wild man
have come to me and said,
surender to true nature.
And live as one with them.
Become one with this earth,
and let love take you in.

Twenty Fifteen

A smell so amazing,
the grapes have been crushed.
Lavender, chocolate,
I love you so much.
The wine has been made in this early bright year.
A glass of this wine in the bay, with a cheer.
Imagine a kiss from your lips, it's from heaven.
When our lips finally meet for the very first time,
I'm sure this wine will do us just fine.

Jar

She's stolen my heart,
keeps it in a jar,
next to a wild mushroom
found in the backyard.
She shows me in dreams.
Tells me of her means,
and why we're apart.
The canopy grows all around this true heart.
Hugs and squeezes this normal-sized jar.
So it doesn't go far.
She tells me she loves me,
but she's stuck in the dark.
Where the fog is so heavy, it keeps us apart.
She keeps my heart hidden,
says soon she'll be free,
and here next to me.

Blush

The sun kissed your skin,
it makes your cheeks blush,
absorbing the energy
that loves you so much.
Your eyes' earth-tone beauty,
a smile so, so bright.
I know that I love you
with all of my might.

Sequenced Beat

I see you in the daytime,
and I dream of you at night.
Our paths just cross so frequently,
and I think that's quite all right.
That extra beat you give my heart,
puts a smile upon my face.
I know it's just our frequencies,
we have similar tastes.
There's something about knowing that we have a
connection,
your heart seems to be quite like mine.
Together you and I,
and always you will have me even on a stormy night.
It's something I just cannot fight.
It's always true my heart's with you.
It's something oh so right.

Sand

I looked into a grain of sand,
and still I found your heart.
I found an energy that never falls apart.
The moonlight showed me with the wind
the meaning of our time.
The seed that grows after the fire
will bloom with so much love.
I love you more today and always,
it's something deep inside.
That grain of sand showed such true love,
it's something brought from God.

Autumn Moon

You come and you love me,
like rain loves the land.
My heart keeps on pounding,
when you're holding my hand.
Our love came so natural,
our tune was just right.
Our frequencies matched,
on that autumn moon night.
Something about us,
a key and a lock.
We open the door
to something so pure.
It's love, it's true love,
and you're my *amor*.

My You

The days and the nights,
and always the lagoon.
You gave me all your kisses,
you gave me love in bloom.
Now I drink my coffee,
and the taste just ain't the same.
I had to keep on moving,
our love I shall reclaim.
The little things remind me of your smile,
just so you know.
The sun, the stars, the moon,
and a bottle of Merlot.
I have you in my heart.
I wish to see you soon.
You're always on my mind,
my love, my lovely tune.

Her Style

Something in her style,
her spirit drives me wild.
Something in her smile,
her kiss is my desire.
Something in her eyes,
the green earth, sand, and fire.
Something in her voice,
I'll talk to her for hours.
Something in her heart,
it's my true soul's desire.

Full of Love

I'm falling deep for her,
just a glass of wine.
She's told me lovely stories,
her heart seems to be mine.
She speaks about the human soul
and the way our love is whole.
We share a bottle called Syrah.
It's dark and inky, nose so full.
Her energy has me in a trance.
Her love I do adore.
I promise to be with you,
till forever, *mi amor*.

Inside Us

It's been a spring or two,
since I fell in love with you.
My Syrah, oh my Syrah!
It's that passion that you give me,
it's those eyes as dark as night.
It's that energy inside us,
that makes everything all right.
Oh my Syrah, Syrah, Syrah.
Your tones are of the colors
of evening on this earth.
Your energy is magic,
that comes straight from the moon.
Your voice is my desire.
I wish to see you soon.
Oh my Syrah, oh my Syrah!
It's love, a lovely tune.

Barcelona

An English señorita living in the Spanish sun.
The magic of the city has her staying oh so long.
I met her in the evening, stating, I won't stay too long.
A week is all I'll be here in the Barcelona sun.
I noticed that she's lovely, and her eyes have said it all.
We spent some time together, and I got to know her soul.
I'm back in California, and I think of her today.
She messaged me and asked how is it out there in the bay.
She can't wait till I go back. She wants to see me now.
A second home is calling, it's a Spanish lovely sound.

Misty Day

The mist keeps coming in,
and the rain just won't let go.
The window's getting foggy,
there's a raincoat on the floor.
Just staring out the window,
and the porch light's getting dim.
I pour myself some Mezcal with a perfect salted rim.
I think about you, darling,
and I have an instant grin.
I miss our days from long ago.
A flashback, daydreaming.
Your voice that's just so charming,
I can still hear it today.
Oh, look, the sun is coming out,
a perfect rainy day.

Always Knew

The moment we kissed,
I knew it was true.
The moonlight came later.
My world was with you.
There's trust and connection,
your love and my heart.
The rooftop, the wine,
the signs from above.
A love meant to be,
it's you and it's me.
I'll hold you forever,
my lovely lady.

Wishbone

Think about something you really want true.
Think about something for me and for you.
Think about happy, think about glad.
Think of the stars that never are sad.
Make the wish and may it come true.
I'll make the wish that you're never blue.

Sparkling Wine

Just a taste, elegant yet wild.
This bottle was different,
a bottle I don't drink much of.
She's sparkling wine, bubbly and explosive,
sweet and sour with hints of wildflower.
I can't wait to have her and see her again.
When she left, I felt it.
I tried a beer, brandy, and wine,
but the satisfaction couldn't compare.
I'm afraid I'm madly in love
with this sunshine-colored
bottle of sparkling wine.

Water Flower

There's a feeling that I'm after,
in the flowers and the rain.
The kisses that you give me
are, of course, my favorite thing.
I can see into the future
when we're dancing in the rain.
Just your eyes, and then your laughter,
and my love for you is claimed.

Can You

Can you dream of light tonight?
The sun will shine this dreamy night.
The air is fresh, the moon is bright.
Can you dream of light tonight?
The birds will chirp this dreamy night,
their hearts will beat for you tonight.
Can you dream of light tonight?

May Flower

There's flowers in your eyes,
an earth tone to my surprise.
Just one Lilly's all I see.
Just a flower being free.
With a charm I can't explain.
I'm feeling something I can't tame.
It's an energy within,
like a half is whole again.
Just a light upon the dark,
and your voice into my heart.
My soul feels there's something here.
I'm in love with you, my dear.

Came Thunder

The hawk screamed his heart out.
The rain came shortly after.
The storm was so damn great,
the hawk seemed like its master.
Thunder came along.
The more he screamed came thunder.
His eyes could tell a story,
of heartache, thunder, and thunder.
He must have lost his love,
he let out all his throb.
His rhythm in the air.
And lightning and more thunder.
A power of the Almighty.
The tears of rain came down.
Tonight the storm has come,
there's lightning and there's thunder.
He misses his true love.
There's lightning up above.
The hawk is bringing lightning,
for his heart, for his true love.

My Lady

If you take my heart hostage,
never let it go.
I'll love you for forever,
I just want you to know.
Love me so deeply
with your heart and all your soul.
And tell me that you'll never let me go.
I'm speaking to you, my darling,
you know. I want you forever,
so don't let me go.

Beauty

Beauty surrounds me wherever I go.
Look from the heavens, earth down below.
The wind carries tales of wonder and bliss.
Surrounded by love, dreams from above.
Dream of the heavens, you holding my hand.
Just close your eyes, and you'll understand.

Love

I allow me to be me, I allow me to be free.
I allow me to be everything I really want to be.
The winds, the sand, the waters too,
they heal my soul, I think of you.
Refreshing rivers, the sun too.
Now here's some love from me to you.
The sand is warm, good to the soul.
I see your eyes, a kiss so full.
I think we're magnets, love of mine.
It's a strange feeling when we're apart.
I think of nothing but your heart.

Of Light

She's a flower,
and she's also a queen.
I'm her protector,
her man and her king.
I remember the night
I gave her my soul.
She gave me her heart,
and oh so much more.
Her eyes are of beauty,
dark as the night.
The energy's wisdom,
of love and of light.

Champagne

She tells me her truth.
Her lips keep on moving,
her accent is smooth.
She looks to my eyes,
she tells me she loves me.
With a glass full of wine.
The stars keep on shining,
a night set so fine.
We're brought together
by God and this wine.
I kiss her lips.
It was sparkling wine.

True Love

I lost myself just yesterday,
a dream showed me the way.
It's been a journey for sometime.
My heart, my mind, my day and day.
I seem to miss you, my true love.
You've been so good to me.
My soul it yearns, and I need more,
I'm just so far away.
May life bring us back real soon.
The sun, the beach, a lovely tune.
I miss your kisses, my true love.
The stars will guide us.
Love is love.

Caught My Eye

I barely even met you,
yet your eyes seem nothing new.
Your smile is something I've known.
I stopped and looked at you.
I felt a real connection
when I looked into your eyes.
I wondered what it can be.
An energy so free,
maybe, maybe, maybe.

Chardonnay

I tasted a few wines today,
some Pinot and Merlot.
The Chardonnay was special,
with a balance, so you know.
We spoke about her interest.
That Merlot gave her a smile.
I'll kiss her lips with no denial.
That Chardonnay, I like her style.
To be in love, a gift from up above.
Oh, señorita love is love.
A glass of wine, a smile.

Ocean Breeze

I just kinda love her,
and the little things she does.
The ocean breeze just moved her hair,
it does just what it does.
There's something in her soul
that I know so very well.
It's something that is good
and always very fair.
Her lips are my desire,
her voice gives me a smile.
And when we sit under the stars,
she hugs me tight.
I know this love has might.
I love you, darling.
Sand and stars,
forever, love is ours.

Midnight Kiss

I look into her eyes,
they're as dark as the night sky.
There's a twinkle and a sparkle like the stars
but they're her eyes.
She smiles and gives me kisses.
She brings happiness to me.
Her cheeks I do adore.
She's my love, my true *amor*.

Gloria

The land bears fine fruit,
it shows in the wine.
The valley's so fertile,
it's one of a kind.
We grow Chardonnay,
and some Pinot too.
I think I'm in love,
with Gloria, with you.
There's love in the flowers,
the wine comes on through.
She lives on the hill,
a sparkling wine.
She's also a beauty,
and one of a kind.

God gave us heaven,
and lots of good wine.

Something of the Soul

I spoke to God today,
I asked for his protection.
May day and night come easy.
May the flowers sing a tune.
I told him of my troubles,
asked to take good care of you,
to always keep you safe.
The sun, the stars, the moon.
My lovely señorita,
it's something of the soul.
I've known you for forever,
since the time of our one Lord.
I love you for forever.
Granada was our home.

That Bottle

It's that wine, it's Cabernet,
the one that made us smile.
It's that bottle of rosé,
that was with us for a while.
It's that wine and our first kiss.
Darling, I do love your style.
It's that wine we had that time,
when we acted pretty wild.
It's a staple to our lives,
it's the culture of the wise.
It's the color, it's the flavor,
it's the spirit that's inside.

And a Glass of Wine

I'm thirsty for your lovin'.
Just a kiss and some Merlot.
To spend my day with you,
just us and us alone.
To speak about the flowers
and your favorite kind of things.
To walk along the coast
and to tease you, pretty thing.
To lay out on the beach
and to always hold your hand.
I love you, lovely lady.
The coast, our love, the sand.
And a little glass of wine,
forever hold my hand.

Daydreamer

My spirit flows in familiar rivers,
while the fresh wind heals my soul.
The creek water fulfills my thirst.
My spirit sleeps on the grassy knoll.
I hang around on old oak trees,
watching life as its story goes.
The bees, the trees, and all the leaves,
are always with me, so I'm never alone.
While the bay tree whispers lullabies,
I look around for river stones.
My heart's forgotten, I have died.
I've passed away, my spirit flies.

Love Forever

When I give you my heart,
keep it for forever.
I know that I'll love you
in all types of weather.
Your eyes I do adore.
Your smile has kissed my soul.
Our paths are the same,
our love we shall claim.
Be strong, and I'll be stronger.
I love you by my side.
You'll always have my love,
a kiss, a wine, and peace of mind.
I'll kiss you for forever
till the end of time.

Even in Snow

Can I love you for the rest of my life?
Can you tell me that you'll never let me go?
Even when the rain is heavy,
or there's lots of snow.
I'm telling you, darling.
I want you to know,
I'm in it for forever and forever,
just so you know.

Henna

Henna, love all through her body.
Incense lit, she calls me darling.
Scarf that drags onto the floor.
Lip balm, mango, tastes like home.
She slides beside me oh so smooth.
She's up against me, beating in tune.
Just a whisper, love me soon.

Moonlight

I miss the Spanish moments
under the full moonlight.
Granada, oh Granada!
The passion of the night.
Señorita dance flamenco.
Just one more glass of wine.
The energy is magic,
the guitar sound is right.
Her lips are crimson red.
She smiles and nods her head.
We speak about the hour,
and the power of the soul.
Her eyes are blue with beauty.
I call her, *mi amor*.

Take Me Back

I admire her body
and look to her soul.
Her color is ruby,
my eyes see Merlot.
Her scent brings me back
to a place I call home.
A moment in time
back in old Mexico.
The first kiss was magic,
it was up on the roof.
The wine we were pouring
was fine and real smooth.
It had us both smiling,
we were finally home.
She whispers she loves me
all the way to the moon.

Nothing New

I'm made from a thousand pebbles,
rocks and boulders too.
The water heals my soul.
I start thinking of you.
My darling, it's your eyes.
Our souls that are so wise.
I've known you for forever
since the spark that lit the sky.
Our God that came from heaven
introduced me to you.
We're sand and sun and water,
our love is nothing new.

Flower Dreamer

She's a flower dreamer, she's so sweet.
The sun sprinkles her with freckles,
when she's dancing in the street.
Like little kisses all around,
this señorita is a delight.
She's a beauty in the sun,
wearing flowers as a crown.
And she always makes me smile,
a perfect lady with some style.
Flower dreamer, I like you,
and I hope you like me too.

Full Glass

You're made from the finest grapes on the vine.
Perfection, my darling, you're doing just fine.
One sip from you, and I smile with delight.
The warmth that you bring me is good to my mind.
To speak with you, darling, is hearts tied with twine.
This thirst that you give me is a glass full of wine.
Our taste is the same, and that's why you're mine.

Midnight Sky

The wind moves the branches, the canopy too.
I'm walking along and start thinking of you.
The night brings the stars, and I look toward the sky.
I look through the clouds, and I do see your eyes.
I hear just a drum, and the wind says hello.
The moon gives me light, just a kiss on the go.
Those dark, dark, dark eyes have done it to me.
They're everything, everywhere and all I can see.

My Soul

I kept looking, I found my soul.
Along with it, my heart rooted,
wrapped around the rocky floor.
In the woods and near the sea,
my love, my darling prays for me.
Her heart guides me, I'm okay.
She's my balance, day by day.

Eyes of Love

Your eyes reflect the colors
of the earth I stand upon.
I can stare into your soul,
forever and forever, we are one.
I think about our love
and the mountains we have climbed.
I think about the ocean
and its waters every time.
Your kisses make me happy,
I can feel them every day.
I love you, pretty lady.
It is always you and I
for forever and forever.
You're my queen, and I'm your guy.

Be

The truth is said so many times
over a glass of wine.
Make sure it's lovely, heavy too.
A blend of magic that loves you.
The thought that lives within the mind.
A glass of wine to be refined.
To share, to love, have a good time.
So when you want to let it be,
enjoy a glass and you shall see.

Late Night

My restless soul bounces off walls
as if I'm missing something.
It's late at night, and
I feel as if I need to finish a conversation
I haven't started.
I'm awake as if something amazing waits for me
tomorrow.
The feeling is something,
something hard to explain.
I do miss her, whoever she is.
I do need her, wherever she may be.
She's not someone I know.
She's not a stranger.
She's love, she's passion.
She's my *amor*.

With You

I've made mistakes
by not knowing what to do.
I've learned, my darling,
my heart is here for you.
If you forgive me and know my heart is true,
we'll conquer all.
I know my heart loves you, I feel it.
And I've also thought it through.
I know I can be forever just with you.

In January

I fell in love with you sometime in January,
or maybe it was June or even February.
The whole damn year, I loved you,
my lovely pretty lady.
My heart just liked you a whole lot
when we were on the ferry.
Driving to the beach, going to the fair,
and looking at some art,
that's when you took my heart.
Going up the mountain, looking at the bay.
Looking at your eyes, my love is here to stay.

Dancing Hawk

The redtails dance in the sky.
They fly through the heavens,
for you and for I.
The wind gently whispers,
she'll always be true.
I hold her hand,
and she squeezes mine too.
A kiss on the cheek.
I adore you, my love.
True nature is us.
We're falling in love.

My Darling

I think I'm falling deep for her,
she's always on my mind.
I feel that she's so close to me,
yet she's an hour drive.
I want to hold her all the time,
it's like my soul has thirst.
She's got the lips I'm looking for,
her eyes, her smile, her nose.
There's something in the way she is,
and I want her more and more.
There's something in the smile she gives.
I want to hug her soul.

Always

I can feel our hearts beat,
two energies flowing.
To have that balance,
is to know we are growing.
Our love keeps on showing.
I love you today,
tomorrow, and always.

Blended

Our souls go together
like a perfect blended wine.
I'm Cabernet and she's Syrah.
I love her for all time.
With hints of flowers and some earth.
Our love is of a kind.
The power that's inside us,
a perfect blended wine.
It's something natural and so strong.
Forever love of mine, I kiss your lips,
our love, one of a kind.

To Kiss You

Your kiss, your eyes,
and a bottle of Merlot.
Just a bit of sugar,
is what I'm looking for.
Blue eyes, blue eyes, blue eyes.
You know, you know, you know.

Perfect Blend

Not just any bottle,
she's the perfect one.
Call her *vino tinto*,
her vibes are of the sun.
Her color is of beauty,
her lips are crimson red.
I drink her and I notice,
the stars align again.
Her heart is my desire,
a bottle of a blend.
I cannot wait to see her
and hold her once again.

Flower Heart

She's got the heart of a flower,
and soul of a queen.
She's from the South,
where I've had many dreams.
I met her in sunshine.
Now I'm back to my home.
I'm from a valley,
that is very well known.
It's autumn, it's chilly,
the leaves all fall down.
It's fall, my darling.
A sound, what a sound.
The wind's getting colder,
and winter's next door.
I'm thinking of her,
my one true *amor*.

My Syrah

The bottle is Syrah,
she's known me for a while.
She knows my heart and soul.
Her lips, a gentle smile.
We spoke about the nothing
and the something for some time.
That wine brought us together.
Yes, her heart seems to be mine.
It's something in her soul,
a balance, and we're whole.
She just fits so damn perfect
in my life, just so you know.
May we always be protected,
may this love last for all time.
Her eyes so dark of beauty,
it's Syrah, Syrah, Syrah.

Sky Flower

I'd like to know your secrets
when I look into your eyes.
I want to kiss your lips.
Blue eyes, blue eyes, blue eyes.
Can you tell me what you think of?
Is it love and fate or hope?
I can show you so much beauty.
It's this world, you know, you know.
It's a dream that brings me wisdom,
it's a flower with a bee.
It's that energy inside us,
when you start thinking of me.
I can read you very well,
and I know you read me too.
We've been spoken of forever,
it's an energy of two.

Dream

The night is cool, refreshing air.
When you're in bed,
may the moon share with you
its dreams of sunny skies.
So you can bathe in sunny rays.

Lucia

She notices the little things
in the flowers, in the trees.
Her energy is wisdom,
wrapped in the colors of the leaves.
The music is flamenco,
she has a lovely sound.
The wine is Tempranillo,
her eyes are a light brown.
The color of her nails,
are a red-orange to me.
She whispers that she loves me,
and she feels the energy.
I'll kiss her for forever,
and forever she's my queen.

Wildflower

Just a flower in the garden,
wild as it can be.
Listen to the wind,
and the waters that you see.
The earth, so rich with minerals,
it's here for you and me.
The energies are wild,
I see what I can see.
A feeling of the heart,
it says to never part.
The sureness of my soul,
knows I love you more and more.

Crimson Rose

Just a whisper to give you a flower of crimson red.
With inner white petals, an aroma of wild fresh
earthiness.

Hints of smoke from a fine cigar.

Listen closely,
and one can perceive this rare flower play of a wonderful
tune.

The stars sing and dance on this foggy moon.

This flower carries the energy of a wonderland,
and that is what I give to you.

Of Cabernet

Energy runs through my veins.
The color's Cabernet,
the lipstick that you wear,
and the rose I gave you
when you thought I really didn't care.
All match this deep, deep color.
I want to say to you,
when we're broken down to particles,
our souls are nothing new.
Two puzzle pieces matching.
Two hearts beat,
night and day.
I'd like to kiss you, darling.
My love for Cabernet.

Her Lips

She didn't say a word,
she's only a bottle.
She loved me at one point.
When I spent time with her.
Damn I shouldn't care,
I also shouldn't swear.
She just tastes so damn good.
I put my mind at ease,
by trimming flowers for the bees.
I chatted with some friends.
I hiked and biked,
and hit the gym with all my might.
But still I think of her,
when I'm alone at night.
Her taste is such delight.
I'm waiting for her message,
but nothing has come through.
It's getting late,
and I admit, I'm a fool for you.

Till Forever

I miss being in love with you.
The sparkling wine gives bubbles.
The summer's almost over,
I want to be at home.
I think about the ocean
and the sand and all its gold.
I think about your kisses,
and the wine that's from Bordeaux.
I've noticed so much passion,
and I just can't get away.
May life and all its pieces
fit right for us today.
I always wish you well
and protect you with my might.
If God allows and guides us,
I'll open up that wine.
And love you till forever,
till the end of time.

Your Eyes

I see the stars above,
and I also see your eyes.
My heart can see it all,
the soul knows what it's looking for.
It's not the sparkling wine,
or the signs I see
that take my mind.
It's embedded in my soul.
That I've known you since so long ago.
It's everything about you.
It's your eyes as dark as night.
It's your voice,
when you say that you love me.
It's an energy that stands so strong.
It's the world that makes real sense.
It's our souls, it's happiness.

Let It Rain

The water keeps on coming,
and I thank God for the rain.
It might be something sad,
but it takes away the pain.
Refreshing are the tears,
it clears the mind.
The grapevines and the olives
can drink this holy rain.
They've been without this water for some time
so let it rain.

I'd Say

I learned to talk to God.
I've shown him all my cards.
He's not the kind who keeps them
and shows them all around.
He helps me to be strong,
and to keep on moving on.
He helps me night and day.
When the chips are low, I pray.
And also, I give thanks
to what he's brought to me.
All the little things,
that make me be the me,
that can see so many ways.
To keep on building up,
an energy, a thought.
And all along,
it's love that comes my way.
It was written in a story,
in the heavens, I would say.

Blue Sky

I want you here, my darling.
I want you by my side.
I tell you it's the stars
and the moon that kiss the sky.
It's getting close to winter,
and I'd like to see your smile.
I keep on climbing higher,
to reach for you and I.
I want to give you roses
and kiss you once or twice.
I must be kidding, darling.
I'll kiss you like ten times,
and share with you my Riesling,
and take you to the show.
It's getting close to winter,
your eyes are what I know.

Color of Syrah

Her eyes are like Syrah,
so dark and almost inky.
She kissed me for a while,
it started with a smile.
I gave her crimson roses,
I took her heart away.
She's got something about her,
that makes me want to stay.
I kissed her in the vineyard
on that February day.
We fit.
I think we're perfect,
in our own imperfect way.

Aura Blue

I fell into a deep sleep,
I was dreaming of the rain.
The moonlight hugged and kissed me.
She whispered out my name.
She gives us light and passion,
and I send her to you.
I tell her all about life
and everything I do.
And she always shines on through.
The moon, the sun, the earth
are all a part of one.
It's an energy that draws me.
A heartbeat on and on.
A flower with an eagle,
a pen and paper too.
The mountains we keep climbing.
Your eyes, they're just so you.
A lady with an aura
of the color blue.

For You

When I looked into her eyes,
I noticed something new.
At the same time,
it's a feeling of knowing her soul too.
Her eyes, they have a birthmark.
Her eyes are just so blue.
I can tell that I do like her,
like a wine under the moon.
A kiss for you, my darling,
and a couple roses too.
I've got you, lovely lady.
The sun, the stars, the moon.

For All Time

I can feel the soul awaken,
when I have a sip of wine.
The kiss is from the heavens.
Her eyes are blue and shine.
I can feel the breeze,
it hugs me, and loves me every time.
I can feel the sunrays kiss me,
I feel the warmth inside.
And when the path is rocky,
I climb and climb and climb.
The building blocks to greatness.
And I have a sip of wine.
The sun, it keeps on shining,
today and for all time.

Cabernet to Merlot

I had a sip of wine,
it was blended with Merlot.
Her soul and I do match.
The stars, they told me so.
I believe in all that jazz,
that's just the way things go.
Sometimes the paths are written,
and some go with the flow.
She's bright, and she is lovely.
Her taste is like Merlot.
Her eyes are filled with magic.
I climb and climb, I soar.
Trying to reach much higher.
I'm here for you, my darling.
I'm Cab to your Merlot.

Señorita Blue

Her eyes are full with magic,
with a birthmark and so blue.
I must have known her soul
back in Spain or in Peru.
I ran into her eyes in mid-October too.
I tell you, señorita,
I'm here waiting for you.
My life, it keeps on moving.
No worries, just be you.
Just keep me close
and say hellos.
Now time can only tell.
I do roll dice,
just once or twice,
for you to be my girl.

Moon Blend

I'm looking for a wine
that brings balance to the soul.
A wine with eyes of beauty,
and so lovely all in all.
Autumn came and went,
now winter's on our side.
The moonlight keeps on shining.
My glass is filled with wine.
I'll share it with you, darling.
We make a real fine blend.
The vines are well,
they're dormant.
They liven up in spring.
I've got you, lovely lady.
The moon, the sun, the wind.

Tied Souls

Would you lock your heart with mine forever?
Do you love me just that much?
Would you hide that key away forever,
and let our souls be lush?
Can you tell me that it's me you're after,
and things just ain't the same?
Do you feel it in your soul
that you need me every day?
Do your eyes see me in crowded places,
and your heart beats so damn much?
Do your lips desire no one but me,
and you want my loving touch?

Bloomed

God spoke just a few words,
and they bloomed into a garden.
He must have written a book
to create beauty like you.
Your mind, your eyes, your soul,
you're lovely all in all.

Any Coast

I'm your poet from the West Coast.
Your eyes hold me real tight.
Sometimes time moves so slowly,
and I think that's quite all right.
I know this feeling matters,
it's an energy within.
Take your time,
you're something special,
just the very best for me.
I've got roses for your garden
and a bottle of Merlot.
Any town, it doesn't matter,
home is always home.
I've got time for something lovely,
a blissful energy.
Hold me tight and don't let go,
mama, you and me.

I've Got You

I can write a million songs for you.
Darling, I'm your man.
I've been known to write a poem or two,
about life, love, and wine from France.
A Merlot or a Syrah,
and the kisses from your lips.
The ups and downs of life,
and drinking too much damn good wine.
And speaking to my God,
about the journey of the heart.
And howling at the moon
when we are far apart.
Look up at the stars, my love,
and take in that fresh air.
You always have me night and day,
forever on and on.
Darling, you're the one.

My Star

I can choose the stars above me,
or the mermaid in the sea.
I can choose the rose behind me,
but, my love, it would not be.
I realized yesterday that there's something to the soul.
The eyes can see so much,
but the soul can see it all.
You're my mermaid, you're my star.
You're my flower, I'm your bee.
I'm your everything forever.
I'm your man, and you're my queen.

Blue eyes, I have to say.
I chose you, my day and day.

Lily Eyes

Lily's got the eyes of beauty,
a flower in a dream.
Pink umbrellas, clear the sky.
Her smile makes smiles
for you and I.
There's a lovely way to her,
shy and so, so pretty.
Stars and sparkles fill the night.
Her heart, her aura, oh so bright.
Moonlight magic all in one.
Lily's got the style and charm.
She's a flower near a stream.
From a place where grapevines dream,
Lily's stylish like a queen.
Flower power,
dream, dream, dream.

My Maria

It's now the twenties, darling,
and the past is left behind.
The distance ain't a thing,
when your energy's like mine.
The sun is always shining.
It's time, it's just our time.
A couple glasses of rich wine,
a balanced Chardonnay.
To always live with passion,
and protection day and day.
May you always smile so lovely,
even if I'm far away.
A million little things,
the mountains and the snow.
I've got you, lovely lady,
so you know,
just so you know.

Full Wine

I knew you in a past life,
I can feel it all around.
You've always been a fine wine,
so lovely, smooth with charm.
You've kissed my soul, I felt it.
I want you by my side.
I know that you are lovely,
your smile, your eyes, your vibe.
I can let you go forever,
and keep on moving on.
I can win your heart and kiss your lips,
on and on and on.
I can drink a wine, Syrah, Merlot,
a blend so full with Cabernet,
just so you know.
I like you, lovely lady.
Blue eyes, your heart and soul.

Everything

I'll dance with you forever.
May the sun shine, shine, and shine.
It's this force that keeps us bonded,
it's an energy of time.
There is no one on this planet
that can take my heart from you.
I love everything about you,
I love everything you do.
It's your eyes, blue like the sky.
It's your lips, your smile so bright.
It's the spirit that's within us,
it's our love that's oh so right.

Alicia

Her energy is vibrant,
I've looked into her soul.
She's tall and thin,
a bottle that's so full.
I say she reminds me
a bit of Merlot.
Her eyes seem like magic,
a hazelnut glow.

Margot

I like your groovy vibe,
and the way you wear your hair.
I like your flower eyes,
and the way you love to share.
You're more than just your looks,
and your lovely, pretty smile.
You're spirit and you're thunder
and a thought of clear blue skies.
Your wisdom is to me like a flower's to a bee.
I'll talk to you for hours about life and all you see.
Your passion is so great,
and that makes me love you more.
Your beauty is a plus,
but your soul brings out true lust.

Kingdom

You can be my queen, darling.
A flower to a bee.
I invite you to my kingdom,
it's everything you see.
The moon, the stars, the waters,
they're all a part of me.
There's whispers in the air,
an echo through the vines.
The wine, it heals the soul.
In your eyes, I see it all.
With you, there is a balance,
an energy that's full.
I'll kiss your lips,
and make you smile.
A rose for you, *amor*.

My Love to You

When I ask for protection,
I also pray for you.
My words, my true intention,
are coming from the soul.
In my dreams, I can hear clearly,
the wisdom of my God.
I can feel it in my blood,
you warm my heart with love.
It is you that makes me,
a man that knows the way.
With your eyes so blue in color,
my queen, you are today.
It is you that gives me strength.
And I find these words to say,
it's love that's been forever.
It was born so long ago,
and is with us to this day.

Page in the air

Page after page, I want something new.
I have it inside,
what to do, what to do?
I can write of the glory that God gave his Son.
I can write of the earth and the heavens as one.
I can write of your smile and your kisses, *amor*.
The trees that are taller over near the shore.
The owls, the wolves, the panda bears too.
It's raining outside, just look at the moon.
I want to see lightning and dance in the rain.
There's heart and there's passion,
a red rose you'll see,
that gives you the warmth
when you're thinking of me.

Blessed

In my pensive state,
I see it all.
In this vast universe,
to think we are so small.
What we do in day to day,
grows the spirit,
pray and pray.
I can write down all my thoughts,
I can be the one for you.
Love me more,
I love you too.
All my kisses are for you.

Kiss of Wine

To today and then tomorrow,
may the sun shine all the time.
May we see each other's eyes.
May your kiss hit me like wine.
To be strong and then much stronger,
I can build into the sky.
There's an energy about this.
I'm the poet of this time.
You're the beauty of my word,
with a heart that's made of gold.
You're the water to the garden,
to make everything unfold.
May the heavens stand beside us.
May we thrive, and thrive, and thrive,
with a kiss, a hug, and wine.
For forever, for all time.

Light Upon

In the morning, I felt sunshine.
I gave my thanks to God.
And gave thanks to my guides,
on the other side.
I almost fell so deep,
and I thought about my life.
To live, to love, and to be wise.
It's light upon my soul,
and to care just a bit more.
I pray into the heavens,
to give us strength, we soar.
May today and our tomorrow
be what we're looking for.
I'll be the strength,
and you be the *amor.*

Eagles Flower

We can be just like wildflowers
in the garden that you see.
We can fly and touch the sky,
like the eagles in the tree.
We can choose to have the colors
that make us truly free.
Let's give in to Mother Nature.
Let it be, just let it be.

Flower Power

Just a flower in the garden,
wild as it can be.
Listen to the wind,
and the waters that you see.
The earth, so rich with minerals,
it's here for you and me.
The energies are wild,
I see what I can see.
A feeling of the heart,
it says to never part.
The sureness of my soul,
knows I love you more and more.

Lifetimes Ago

The smell after the rain,
is something brought from beauty.
There's forest oak and pines,
eucalyptus soothes my mind.
My soul is made of things
embedded in the forest.
The falcon in the daytime,
and the owl late at night.
I ran into your eyes,
when I looked into the heavens.
Your lips create a feeling
that takes me back,
way back in time.
To that forest, to that place
I knew so long ago.
Your lips are still my favorite.
A thing, our thing, you know.

Leaves

Autumn is here.
The leaves are all changing,
and the water's so clear.
Her eyes are so lovely,
and her smile's still the same.
When I heard her voice,
my love was reclaimed.
Your energy's magic.
I adore you, you see.
And I've noticed
you can't keep your eyes off of me.

My Love

I'm up in the mountains,
with blue skies today.
It's perfectly perfect,
a bright sunny day.
I look at the beauty,
a reminder of you.
An oak with fine character
and spanish moss too.
A beauty in nature,
and you to my heart.
I love you so much.
I'd trade you for nothing.
My heart, my true heart.

Just a Bit

I can see into the past,
when I look into your eyes.
I can see the ships that sailed,
and you picking dandelions.
I could feel the color of your soul,
when I kissed your lips that night.
I can feel we knew each other
from so very long ago.
From a place so far away,
so far away from home.
A place that's called La Rioja.
Where the wine is like the gold.
Just a bit of Tempranillo,
to feel, to feel at home.

In the Rain

I spoke into the rain,
and tuned into the soul.
A million little kisses,
I'm never all alone.
The stars peek through the clouds.
The owls, they seem so tame.
The puddles feed the flowers.
I'm talking to the rain.
I ask for its protection,
and to always keep me strong.
I send out this protection,
to my Dad and to my Mom.
May always and forever
I be the me I am.
The world, it has such beauty.
The eyes of love I claim.

October Blue

I met her in October,
yet it wasn't very cold.
It was in the vineyard,
a place I call my home.
She's something very special.
Her vibe hit my heart's string.
Her voice feels like it's magic,
a very lovely ring.
I feel that she's my queen,
she attracts me like a dream.
There's everything about her,
her eyes, her smile, her means.

The Tone

The tone was so smooth,
a Spanish guitar.
I felt the earth's beat,
a rhythm to the heart.
I'll go with the flow,
that's just what I do.
The stars sometimes guide me,
and they guide you too.
I see you are special,
it's something in you.
I keep climbing mountains,
and I'm writing for two.
I'm here for you, darling.
The sun and the stars.
An eagle with fire,
to light up your heart.

Popcorn

I can write a million poems,
and conquer Earth for you.
I can make a perfect blend,
of wine that's made for two.
I can open every door,
and tease you, my *amor*.
I can show you my whole world,
and take you to the shore.
I can share my drink with you,
a perfect Cabernet.
I'll take you to the movies,
and sneak some Chardonnay.
That goes perfectly perfect,
with the popcorn, movie plays.
I guess I kinda like you,
if I share my Cabernet.

Grapes

I don't know what it is,
but I like that pink Merlot.
Maybe it's the color,
I really do not know.
I had a perfect blend,
but I threw it all away.
Two broken hearts,
a bond of yesterday.
I haven't found a wine
that I wanted more than you.
I keep on moving forward,
and everything's so new.
I tell you, lovely lady,
I'm a Cabernet.
The vineyards keep on growing.
The moon, the sun, the rain,
all in perfect soil.
The heart feels the same way.
I'd like to be your poet,
and you, my pink rosé.

Words of Glue

Simply true, I look for you,
yet I just haven't found you.
A broken heart made up of glue,
some tape and words of
I do love you.
You're everywhere with such great eyes.
I really want to hug you.
One look from you
and to my surprise,
darling, I do love you.

Under the Stars

I share my popcorn with you,
I also share my wine.
But at dinner, pretty lady,
the cushy seat is mine.
I give you all my kisses,
thousands, I can say.
I love your eyes, my darling.
The city by the bay.
We drive up to the mountain,
and look up at the moon.
The ocean waves are soothing.
We speak about a tune.
We chat about the past,
and kiss under the stars.
My lovely señorita,
this whole night, it's all ours.

You and I

I sleep and I dream.
You're thinking of me.
I know it's so true,
that energy's you.
I look in your eyes,
and I see so much passion.
We walk and we talk,
and we both must want something.
When I wake, it's so vague,
and I go with my day.
Then a trigger is felt,
and I feel the same way.
I start to remember,
and I'm feeling your touch.
I think of how lovely you are,
sunlight blush.

Luck

I was in a dream,
the sky had blended colors.
I looked into a stream,
with turtles, coins, and flowers.
You called my name out twice,
and I looked into your eyes.
You gave me a full glass,
of lemonade with ice.
I gave you two, three kisses,
and I sat down there with you.
We looked into the sky,
and everything felt new.
I remember that your heart
had the same beat as my own.
The rabbits kept on dancing,
and then came out the moon.
I got you, señorita,
I'm as solid as a rock.
We're always well protected
with the energy of luck.

Italian Blend

Just a little coffee,
the smell and taste are great.
I'm looking out the window,
the leaves dance with the wind.
I'm thinking of the next step,
just planning some stuff out.
I keep on seeing signs
of what I'm all about.
This coffee is amazing,
a light Italian blend.
I have so many options.
My heart, my mind, I'm zen.
I want to roll the dice
on someone just like you.
Lady Luck, she loves me,
and there's nothing I can do.

Thoughts of You

I'd like to win your heart today,
and then tomorrow too.
I want to tell you things
that are just for me and you.
Your eyes, they bring such magic.
And I want to kiss you more.
Close your eyes and see the stars,
you're what I'm looking for.
A glass of wine, and all is fine.
It's Pinot, so you know.
It grows in such cool weather,
and it gives me so much warmth.
I thought of you today,
just walking in the vineyards.
I send you peace and love,
from here out to Virginia.

Dry Riesling

I'd like to win your heart today,
and then tomorrow too.
I'm not sure what it is,
but I'm here thinking of you.
Maybe it's your eyes,
like a treasure to the wise.
It's a bottle full of Riesling,
and your smile in the night sky.
It's an energy of spirit,
and the meaning of fine words.
It's the glue of something new.
It's a bottle made for two.
I'll drink a glass tonight,
of that bottle made for you.

Evelyn

I've met a señorita
who charmed me with her eyes.
Her heart is full and caring.
Her eyes, her eyes, her eyes.
Her soul is full of beauty,
I can hear it in her voice.
The smell of lavender,
with a glass of wine so full.
She's a woman who climbs mountains,
and she's something oh so true.
I can see it all around her,
it's an energy so new.
She gives me lovely kisses,
I want to see her more.
She's a queen, I'm her *amor*.

Some Coffee

The line just keeps on blinking,
there's nothing on my mind.
I want to write the lyrics
to a love that's oh so fine.
I see her pretty face,
and her eyes as dark as night.
I have a little coffee,
and I want her by my side.
I'm waiting on a call
to help a friend in motion.
Just on the other side,
going toward the ocean.
I guess I'm writing something
when there's nothing on my mind.
I'd love to kiss your lips, blue eyes.
And the dark, dark eyes I spotted,
just a metaphor for coffee.
Some pretty damn good coffee.

Evening Comes

I kind of want some popcorn
and kisses from your lips.
A little bit of rosé or maybe Chardonnay.
Whatever it may be,
your lips, they're all I see.
A perfect evening, darling.
Just the stars and you and me.
I'll surprise you with some roses,
some chocolate, and some wine.
I've got you, my sweet darling.
I'm yours, and you are mine.

A little More

I'd like to know you a little more today,
just a little more each and every day.
I want to give you roses and take you to a show.
I want to know your thoughts and kiss your lips, *amor*.
To share my popcorn with you and drink some
Chardonnay.
To give you some dark chocolate and see you every day.
Just to get to know you a little bit today.

Pink Wine

I want to hear your heartbeat,
I want to kiss your lips,
I want to hold you close,
and whisper words of bliss.
I like you, my rosé.
I saw it in your eyes,
the beauty that's inside you,
a whisper to the wise.
When I heard your voice,
I felt it, it did something to me.
I tell you, pretty lady,
your eyes are what I see.
I want to see you, darling.
And kiss you more and more.
I'm just a Cabernet,
drawn to you, *amor*.

About the Author

Wine, love, and God.

Jimmy grew up in the California wine country of Sonoma/Napa. With wine in his roots, he fell in love with Merlot, his favorite metaphor. Mixing his passion for wine with romance, he found it easy to express himself in this manner.

He started writing poetry in his early twenties. Inspired by the world around him—music, love, wine, traveling, and friendships—he began to write. Romance was the seed of it all. His passion for writing developed and grew as he experienced the world—digging deep into his roots and finding what he's all about, experiencing the ups and downs of life, learning to speak to God, and finding refuge in the spirit, knowing the soul and the energy of love.

CPSIA information can be obtained
at www.ICGtesting.com
Printed in the USA
BVHW041404111021
618680BV00013B/338